FLORIDA TEST PREP
FAST Reading Skills Workbook
Daily Star Practice
Kindergarten

© 2023 by Franklin Thomas

All rights reserved. No part of this book may be reproduced or transmitted in any form or by any means, electronic, mechanical, photocopying, recording, or otherwise without prior written permission.

ISBN 9798379349547

TEST MASTER PRESS

FAST Reading Skills Workbook, Daily Star Practice, Kindergarten

CONTENTS

Introduction	4
Star Practice Exercises	**5**
Set 1 – Vocabulary	5
Set 2 – Reading Prose and Poetry	19
Set 3 – Reading Informational Texts	29
Set 4 – Vocabulary	39
Set 5 – Reading Prose and Poetry	53
Set 6 – Reading Informational Texts	63
Set 7 – Vocabulary	73
Set 8 – Reading Prose and Poetry	87
Set 9 – Reading Informational Texts	97
Set 10 – Vocabulary	107
Set 11 – Reading Prose and Poetry	121
Set 12 – Reading Informational Texts	131
Answer Key	**141**
Set 1 – Vocabulary	142
Set 2 – Reading Prose and Poetry	144
Set 3 – Reading Informational Texts	146
Set 4 – Vocabulary	148
Set 5 – Reading Prose and Poetry	150
Set 6 – Reading Informational Texts	152
Set 7 – Vocabulary	154
Set 8 – Reading Prose and Poetry	156
Set 9 – Reading Informational Texts	158
Set 10 – Vocabulary	160
Set 11 – Reading Prose and Poetry	162
Set 12 – Reading Informational Texts	164

INTRODUCTION
For Parents, Teachers, and Tutors

About the New Florida Assessment of Student Thinking (F.A.S.T.)

Students in Florida will take the Florida Assessment of Student Thinking (F.A.S.T.). This is a Progress Monitoring System that involves taking tests throughout the school year to show current level and progress. Students in Kindergarten will take the Star Reading test produced by Renaissance Learning. The tests are taken three times throughout the year. This book will prepare students for the Star Reading tests.

About Florida's New English Language Arts Standards

Student learning and assessment in Florida is based on the skills listed in the new Benchmarks for Excellent Student Thinking, or B.E.S.T. The reading standards are divided into three areas: Reading Prose and Poetry, Reading Informational Text, and Reading Across Genres. The Star Reading tests also cover the skills in the Vocabulary section of the standards. This book covers all the reading and vocabulary skills assessed on the test.

Ongoing Skill Development

The aim of this book is to give students ongoing practice with questions like those on the Star tests. Each set focuses on one area. Within each set, there are 4 vocabulary quizzes or 4 reading passages. The questions in each set cover all the B.E.S.T. skills for that area.

By focusing on one passage at a time, students can focus on understanding a passage fully. Students can be guided through the passages and questions one at a time, or can complete them independently and receive feedback after. This format allows for skill development and positive guidance and feedback.

About the Star Reading Tests

The Star Reading tests have students answer multiple-choice questions with three answer choices. The reading questions include a short passage, while the vocabulary questions are stand-alone. This practice book has questions with the same format, except that 5 questions are asked about a passage instead of just one. This reduces the reading demands on young students, while still ensuring that students develop the reading comprehension skills needed.

Star Practice Exercises

Set 1

Vocabulary

Instructions

Read each question carefully.

Each question has three answer choices.

Fill in the circle for the correct answer.

Vocabulary Quiz 1

1 The sky is _____.

Which word goes on the line?

① blue

② cloud

③ day

2 Fish live in _____.

Which word goes on the line?

① grow

② swim

③ water

3   The sun is shining.

What is the base word of *shining*?

① shin

② shine

③ ing

4   It was a chilly winter morning.

Which word means the same as *chilly*?

① cold

② dry

③ long

5   I pushed and I pushed. The door would not <u>budge</u>.

What does *budge* mean?

①   leave

②   move

③   break

6   Read the words below.

      cat
      dog
      flower
      mouse

Which word is not like the others?

①   dog

②   flower

③   mouse

Vocabulary Quiz 2

1 Trees have _____ leaves.

Which word goes on the line?

① green

② grow

③ stems

2 The moon shines at _____.

Which word goes on the line?

① bright

② night

③ sleep

3 Luca played outside.

Which word has the same base word as *played*?

① painting

② playing

③ pushing

4 The joyful puppy wagged his tail.

Which word means the same as *joyful*?

① happy

② little

③ young

5   I was so tired. I nodded off.

What does "nodded off" mean?

① got sick

② fell asleep

③ yelled

6   Read the words below.

blue
green
yellow

Which word could be added to the list?

① sky

② tree

③ red

Vocabulary Quiz 3

1   Flowers are _____ pretty.

       Which word goes on the line?

       ①   nice

       ②   smell

       ③   very

2   Butterflies fly in the _____.

       Which word goes on the line?

       ①   air

       ②   flap

       ③   wings

3 Kim loves <u>dancing</u>.

What is the base word of *dancing*?

① dan

② dance

③ ing

4 The whale was very <u>large</u>.

Which word means the same as *large*?

① big

② loud

③ slow

5   Isla forgot lunch. Isla was <u>hungry</u>.

What does *hungry* tell about Isla?

① She wants to eat.

② She wants to play.

③ She wants to sleep.

6   Read the words below.

apple

moon

star

sun

Which word is not like the others?

① apple

② moon

③ star

Vocabulary Quiz 4

1 Dogs make great _____.

Which word goes on the line?

- ① bark
- ② pets
- ③ loyal

2 The sun rises in the _____.

Which word goes on the line?

- ① east
- ② star
- ③ warm

3 We <u>walked</u> to the shops.

Which word has the same base word as *walked*?

① waiting

② waking

③ walking

4 The rock band was <u>noisy</u>.

Which word means the same as *noisy*?

① free

② good

③ loud

5   The kitten was missing.

What does *missing* mean?

① lost

② soft

③ pretty

6   Read the words below.

bike
car
train

Which word could be added to the list?

① hat

② dog

③ truck

Bonus Vocabulary Practice

Write a sentence using each word listed below.

1. blue

   _____

2. run

   _____

3. little

   _____

4. fun

   _____

Star Practice Exercises

Set 2

Reading Prose and Poetry

Instructions

Read each question carefully.

Each question has three answer choices.

Fill in the circle for the correct answer.

The Hungry Bunny

Once upon a time, there was a little rabbit. He hopped through the forest. He was looking for carrots to eat. He found a big patch. He ate as many as he could.

He was so full that he couldn't hop anymore. He lay down and fell asleep. He dreamed of carrots.

1. Who would have drawn the picture of the rabbit?

    ① author

    ② illustrator

    ③ publisher

2. What does the word *little* tell about the rabbit?

    ① where he is

    ② how he feels

    ③ what he looks like

3 What is the setting of the story?

① a farm

② a forest

③ a zoo

4 What does the rabbit do first?

① falls asleep

② eats lots of carrots

③ has a dream

5 How does the rabbit feel after eating the carrots?

① full

② mad

③ sorry

The Spider and the Caterpillar

Once upon a time, there was a little spider. He was always trying to make friends. One day, he saw a caterpillar. The spider said hello. But the caterpillar was scared and ran away. The spider was very sad. He decided to make a web. When the caterpillar saw the web, he was amazed. The two became best friends.

1 Who wrote the words?

① author

② illustrator

③ reader

2 Which word tells how the caterpillar felt?

① hello

② scared

③ ran

3 How does the spider try to make friends?

    ① He does a dance.

    ② He says hello.

    ③ He plays a game.

4 How does the caterpillar feel when he sees the web?

    ① amazed

    ② sad

    ③ worried

5 What is the story about?

    ① making friends

    ② winning a race

    ③ going somewhere new

Dancing Girl

Sally loved to dance. She would put on her pink tutu every day. She would twirl around the room. She danced everywhere she went. She danced in the park. She danced at school. She danced at the grocery store. She made everyone smile.

1 What was the main job of the author?

① writing the words

② taking the photo

③ checking for mistakes

2 Which word tells how the girl moved?

① tutu

② day

③ twirl

3   When does Sally dance?

   ①   all the time

   ②   on the weekends

   ③   in the mornings

4   Which is not a place that Sally dances?

   ①   in the park

   ②   on the bus

   ③   at school

5   How does the dancing girl make people feel?

   ①   happy

   ②   silly

   ③   mad

Flowers

Flowers are so pretty,
In the garden they grow.
With petals soft and fluffy,
And colors that just glow.

Reds, yellows, pinks, and blues,
Each one is unique and bright.
We pick them for our mommies,
And give them with delight.

1. Which words in the first verse rhyme?

   ① pretty and fluffy

   ② garden and grow

   ③ grow and glow

2. What does the word *soft* tell about the petals?

   ① how they look

   ② how they feel

   ③ how they smell

3   Where are the flowers growing?

① in a pot

② in a garden

③ in a vase

4   Which word means about the same as *glow*?

① change

② shine

③ smell

5   What are the people picking the flowers doing?

① something mean

② something nice

③ something silly

Bonus Vocabulary Practice

Write a sentence using each word listed below.

1. apple

   _____

2. play

   _____

3. look

   _____

4. good

   _____

Star Practice Exercises

Set 3

Reading Informational Texts

Instructions

Read each question carefully.

Each question has three answer choices.

Fill in the circle for the correct answer.

The Moon

The Moon is a big rock. It orbits the Earth. This means it goes around the Earth.

It shines at night. It helps us see in the dark. It looks so lovely.

It also causes the tides. Tides make the ocean rise and fall.

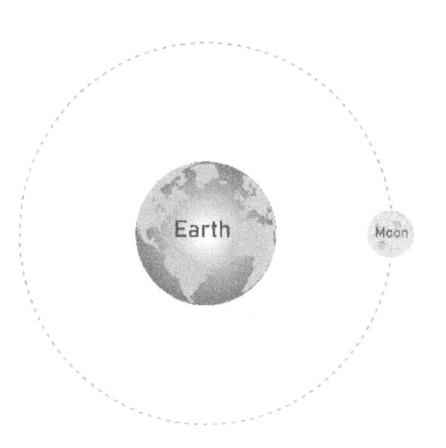

1. What does the art show about the Moon?

   ① It shines.

   ② It orbits.

   ③ It is a rock.

2. What does the Moon cause?

   ① seasons

   ② tides

   ③ wind

3 Which detail about the Moon is an opinion?

① It is a big rock.

② It shines at night.

③ It looks lovely.

4 What does the word *big* tell about the Moon?

① its color

② its shape

③ its size

5 Which paragraph tells how the Moon moves?

① Paragraph 1

② Paragraph 2

③ Paragraph 3

How to Brush Your Teeth

1. Wet your toothbrush.

2. Squeeze toothpaste on the toothbrush.

3. Brush your teeth up and down, left and right, and all around.

4. Spit out the toothpaste. Rinse your mouth.

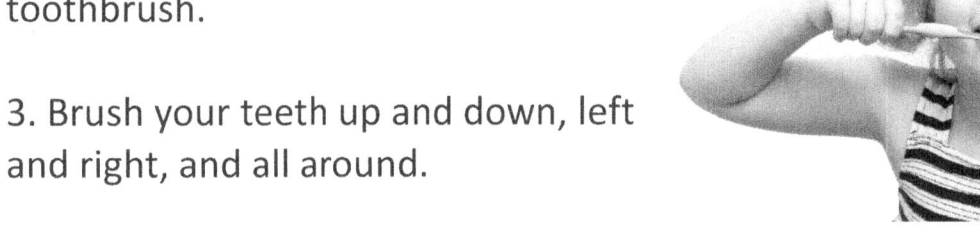

Brushing is fun!

1   What does the picture show?

   ①   the main character

   ②   the setting

   ③   the topic

2   What is the text doing?

   ①   giving an opinion

   ②   teaching something

   ③   telling a story

3 The text says that brushing is fun. What is this?

① a fact

② an opinion

③ a question

4 Which step tells how to move the toothbrush?

① Step 1

② Step 2

③ Step 3

5 What is the last thing you do?

① brush

② rinse

③ spit

About My Job

I am a teacher. I help students learn new things. I use books and videos to teach. We learn to read and write. We learn our numbers. We also have lots of fun. We do art and play music. Teaching makes me happy.

1. What does the picture show?

    ① doing art

    ② learning numbers

    ③ playing music

2. What is the text about being?

    ① a friend

    ② a sister

    ③ a teacher

3   Which detail is an opinion?

   ①   We learn to read and write.

   ②   We learn our numbers.

   ③   We also have lots of fun.

4   Which word tells how the teacher feels?

   ①   learn

   ②   play

   ③   happy

5   What does the teacher use to help students learn?

   ①   books and videos

   ②   rhymes and songs

   ③   tests and quizzes

Let's Put On Sunscreen

It's hot outside. Let's go and play. Wait a minute! There's something we need to do. We need to put on sunscreen.

We should always wear sunscreen when we go outside. It protects our skin from the sun's rays. If we don't wear it, we might get a sunburn. Ouch! So, let's put on sunscreen before we head out!

1 What does the title show about the text?

① It is a true story.

② It gives facts.

③ It tells people what to do.

2 What is the text about?

① being safe outside

② having fun outside

③ not going outside

3 Which sentence tells what sunscreen does?

① We should always wear sunscreen when we go outside.

② It protects our skin from the sun's rays.

③ So, let's put on sunscreen before we head out!

4 What does the word *hot* tell about outside?

① how it feels

② how it looks

③ how it smells

5 What might you get if you don't put on sunscreen?

① headache

② runny nose

③ sunburn

Bonus Vocabulary Practice

Write a sentence using each word listed below.

1. moon

_____

2. car

_____

3. hat

_____

4. stop

_____

Star Practice Exercises

Set 4

Vocabulary

Instructions

Read each question carefully.

Each question has three answer choices.

Fill in the circle for the correct answer.

Vocabulary Quiz 1

1 The cat is _____.

Which word goes on the line?

① pet

② purr

③ sleeping

2 Apples are a _____ snack.

Which word goes on the line?

① crunch

② great

③ grow

3 I have a <u>skipping</u> rope.

What is the base word of *skipping*?

① ski

② skip

③ ing

4 The <u>damp</u> grass felt cold.

Which word means the same as *damp*?

① dry

② new

③ wet

5 It was late. I was <u>sleepy</u>.

What does *sleepy* mean?

① lost

② sore

③ tired

6 Read the words below.

cold

hat

hot

warm

Which word is not like the others?

① hat

② hot

③ warm

Vocabulary Quiz 2

1 Sarah is _____ with her dolls.

Which word goes on the line?

① fun

② playing

③ girls

2 The bird is singing _____.

Which word goes on the line?

① nicely

② parrot

③ tree

3 Ellen reads every day.

Which word has the same base word as *reads*?

① leading

② reading

③ redo

4 The bike moved quickly down the hill.

Which word means the same as *quickly*?

① fast

② loud

③ rough

5   Ella is five. She cannot take the bus <u>alone</u>.

What does *alone* mean?

① for free

② by herself

③ with a friend

6   Read the words below.

down
left
up

Which word could be added to the list?

① cat

② rock

③ right

Vocabulary Quiz 3

1 The boy jumped so _____.

Which word goes on the line?

① high

② skipped

③ happy

2 Mia loves to _____.

Which word goes on the line?

① dance

② dancing

③ danced

3 I washed my clothes.

What is the base word of *washed*?

① was

② wash

③ shed

4 The rain made me feel gloomy.

Which word means the same as *gloomy*?

① cold

② joy

③ sad

5 The play will <u>begin</u> at 5 o'clock.

What does *begin* mean?

① end

② rest

③ start

6 Read the words below.

> fast
> quick
> slow
> snail

Which word is not like the others?

① quick

② slow

③ snail

Vocabulary Quiz 4

1   The wind is _____.

Which word goes on the line?

① blowing

② trees

③ storm

2   Amelia enjoys baking _____.

Which word goes on the line?

① cookies

② yummy

③ kitchen

3 I <u>looked</u> for my lost cat.

Which word has the same base word as *looked*?

① looking

② lucky

③ took

4 The bridge is <u>sturdy</u>. It has stood for years.

Which word means the same as *sturdy*?

① busy

② heavy

③ strong

5	"Get out of here," Mike shouted.

What does *shouted* mean?

① hoped

② raced

③ yelled

6	Read the words below.

walk

run

jump

Which word could be added to the list?

① hop

② boat

③ house

Bonus Vocabulary Practice

Write a sentence using each word listed below.

1. fish

_____

2. green

_____

3. home

_____

4. lost

_____

Star Practice Exercises

Set 5

Reading Prose and Poetry

Instructions

Read each question carefully.

Each question has three answer choices.

Fill in the circle for the correct answer.

The Rainbow

Susie loved to paint. She would paint pictures of flowers and trees. One day, she painted a rainbow. It took her a long time. It was so colorful. She showed it to her father. He liked it very much. He put it in a frame and hung it on the wall.

1   Who wrote the words?

   ①   author

   ②   illustrator

   ③   Susie

2   Which word tells how the rainbow looked?

   ①   long

   ②   time

   ③   colorful

3 Where does Susie's father put the picture?

① in a frame

② on the fridge

③ on his desk

4 What is the story about?

① Susie's school

② Susie's hobby

③ Susie's pets

5 What does the father think about the picture?

① It is silly.

② It is sad.

③ It is special.

The Farmer and the Bird
by Paula Jones

Once upon a time, there was a lazy bird. He wanted to find an easy way to get food. He didn't want to hunt for it. One day, the bird had an idea. He saw a farmer planting seeds. The bird followed the farmer. He ate all the seeds the farmer planted. The poor farmer did not see the bird. He never found out why his plants did not grow.

The End

1 Which tells who wrote the words?

① The Farmer and the Bird

② by Paula Jones

③ The End

2 Which word tells what the bird is like?

① lazy

② easy

③ poor

3   What does the bird do to get food?

   ①   eats worms

   ②   takes the seeds

   ③   asks the farmer

4   What is the story about?

   ①   a bird being naughty

   ②   a farmer being smart

   ③   some seeds being magic

5   Who would be happy in the story?

   ①   only the bird

   ②   only the farmer

   ③   the bird and the farmer

The Flashlight

Timmy was afraid of the dark. He liked to sleep with the light on. One night, his mother helped him. She turned off the lights. Then she gave Timmy a flashlight. She showed him how to use it. Timmy sat it beside his bed. Timmy wasn't afraid anymore.

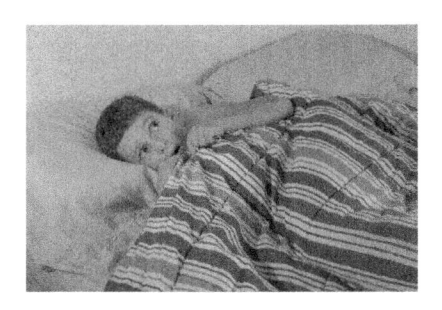

1   What did the author mainly do?

① take the photo

② check for mistakes

③ write the words

2   Which sentence tells where Timmy puts the flashlight?

① She showed him how to use it.

② Timmy sat it beside his bed.

③ Timmy wasn't afraid anymore.

3 What is Timmy afraid of?

① monsters

② storms

③ the dark

4 What is Timmy's mother like?

① helpful

② cheerful

③ scared

5 What is the story about?

① a boy making a new friend

② a boy getting over a fear

③ a boy learning a new skill

The Sun

The sun is big and yellow,
It shines up in the sky.
It warms us and it helps us grow,
With its bright and shining light.

We have fun when it's sunny,
And play outside all day.
But when the night comes,
The sun goes away.

1 Which word rhymes with *day*?

① sunny

② outside

③ away

2 Which word tells what the sun looks like?

① yellow

② sky

③ warms

3 What do the children do when it's sunny?

① have a nap

② go swimming

③ play outside

4 What does the poet say the sun is like?

① bright

② round

③ happy

5 What does the picture show?

① how kids play in the sun

② how hot the sun is

③ how the sun goes away

Bonus Vocabulary Practice

Write a sentence using each word listed below.

1. sun

_____

2. fast

_____

3. tree

_____

4. cake

_____

Star Practice Exercises

Set 6

Reading Informational Texts

Instructions
Read each question carefully. Each question has three answer choices. Fill in the circle for the correct answer.

Birds

A bird is an animal. Birds have feathers and wings. Most birds can fly. Birds have different songs. The songs can be lovely. Birds use their beaks to eat. They also use them to build nests.

1. What does the photo show a bird doing?

   ① eating

   ② flying

   ③ singing

2. What do birds use to eat?

   ① beaks

   ② feathers

   ③ wings

3 What is the text doing?

① telling a story

② giving an opinion

③ telling facts

4 The texts says that "the songs can be lovely." What does this describe?

① sights

② sounds

③ smells

5 What do birds do?

① build nests

② dig holes

③ make dams

How to Plant a Flower

1. Get a pot and some soil.

2. Put soil in the pot.

3. Take a seed. Carefully place it in the soil.

4. Put it in a sunny spot.

5. Water the plant every few days. The soil should be damp.

There are lots of types of flowers. I like roses best. Pick the one you like best.

1 What does the title show the text is about?

　① buying flowers

　② giving flowers

　③ growing flowers

2 When should the plant be watered?

　① every morning

　② every few days

　③ once a week

3   The author says she likes roses best. What is this?

① a fact

② an opinion

③ a question

4   What does the word *damp* tell?

① how the soil feels

② how the soil smells

③ how the soil tastes

5   What do you do first?

① get a pot

② plant a seed

③ water the soil

Henry Ford

Henry Ford was born in 1863. He loved working with machines. He started making cars. He made a car called the Model T. He made lots of cars quickly. His cars did not cost much. Now lots of people could buy a car. It was so wonderful. It changed how people lived and worked. He did a great thing!

Henry Ford

1 What is the text?

① a funny story

② a scary story

③ a true story

2 What is the text about?

① Henry Ford's family

② Henry Ford's problems

③ Henry Ford's work

3 Which detail about Henry Ford is an opinion?

① He was born in 1863.

② He made the Model T.

③ He did a great thing.

4 How did Henry Ford make his cars?

① carefully

② quickly

③ slowly

5 What helped lots of people buy a car?

① They were cheap.

② They were small.

③ They were slow.

Playing the Piano

A piano is used to play music. It has keys you press. It can be hard to learn. You must practice often. But it is worth it. Playing the piano is a great skill. The music can sound wonderful. You could even write your own songs!

1 What is the topic of the text?

① music

② school

③ sport

2 What do you press to play a piano?

① buttons

② keys

③ strings

3 Which sentence is a fact?

① A piano is used to play music.

② You must practice often.

③ But it is worth it.

4 Which word means the same as *hard*?

① difficult

② fun

③ slow

5 What does the author think about learning the piano?

① It takes too long.

② It is a good skill.

③ It costs a lot.

Bonus Vocabulary Practice

Write a sentence using each word listed below.

1. song

_____

2. walk

_____

3. funny

_____

4. house

_____

Star Practice Exercises

Set 7

Vocabulary

Instructions

Read each question carefully.

Each question has three answer choices.

Fill in the circle for the correct answer.

Vocabulary Quiz 1

1 Birds can fly in the _____.

Which word goes on the line?

① high

② sky

③ wings

2 Emma likes to _____ pictures.

Which word goes on the line?

① draw

② making

③ nice

3 We cooked a nice dinner.

What is the base word of *cooked*?

① clock

② cook

③ close

4 The little mouse ran away.

Which word means the same as *little*?

① brown

② small

③ young

5 Sally was <u>glad</u> to see her aunt.

What does *glad* mean?

① amazed

② happy

③ bored

6 Read the words below.

> big
> giraffe
> medium
> small

Which word is not like the others?

① giraffe

② medium

③ small

Vocabulary Quiz 2

1 The fish swims in the _____.

Which word goes on the line?

① blue

② fins

③ lake

2 I like to play _____.

Which word goes on the line?

① outside

② climb

③ friends

3 The trash was <u>smelly</u>.

Which word has the same base word as *smelly*?

①   smaller

②   smelling

③   seller

4 I sat under the tree. I had a <u>snooze</u>.

Which word means the same as *snooze*?

①   meal

②   nap

③   idea

5   I put the <u>final</u> piece in the puzzle.

What does *final* mean?

① last

② nice

③ small

6   Read the words below.

dry
hot
wet

Which word could be added to the list?

① cold

② milk

③ rabbit

Vocabulary Quiz 3

1 We saw animals at the _____.

Which word goes on the line?

① lion

② snakes

③ zoo

2 The giant ate the _____ cake.

Which word goes on the line?

① bake

② gobble

③ whole

3 Connor <u>listened</u> to music.

What is the base word of *listened*?

① light

② list

③ listen

4 The <u>jet</u> flew off into the sky.

Which word means about the same as *jet*?

① ball

② bird

③ plane

5   Tia won the race. She got an <u>award</u>.

What does *award* mean?

① party

② prize

③ smile

6   Read the words below.

day
morning
night
play

Which word is not like the others?

① morning

② night

③ play

Vocabulary Quiz 4

1 The flowers grow in the _____.

Which word goes on the line?

① garden

② roses

③ watering

2 The sand was soft and _____.

Which word goes on the line?

① beach

② castle

③ warm

3 The dog is <u>barking</u>.

Which word has the same base word as *barking*?

① baked

② barked

③ blacker

4 The cat <u>peeked</u> through the hole.

Which word means the same as *peeked*?

① danced

② looked

③ moved

5   Sam tried to <u>repair</u> the old car.

What does *repair* mean?

① change

② fix

③ move

6   Read the words below.

apple
pear
plum

Which word could be added to the list?

① banana

② red

③ home

Bonus Vocabulary Practice

Write a sentence using each word listed below.

1. key

_____

2. fly

_____

3. jump

_____

4. pig

_____

Star Practice Exercises

Set 8

Reading Prose and Poetry

Instructions

Read each question carefully.

Each question has three answer choices.

Fill in the circle for the correct answer.

Friends

A puppy and a kitten became friends. They played together every day. They ran in the park. They chased each other. They shared their toys. They had lots of fun. People thought it was funny to see a dog and a cat playing together.

1. What did the author mainly do?

    ① check for mistakes

    ② take the photo

    ③ write the words

2. Which word tells how the friends move?

    ① ran

    ② park

    ③ toys

FAST Reading Skills Workbook, Daily Star Practice

3 Who is the story about?

① two kittens

② two puppies

③ a puppy and a kitten

4 What do the friends do?

① have a fight

② make plans

③ play together

5 What do people think the friends are like?

① funny

② odd

③ scary

The Tortoise and the Hare

A speedy hare liked to boast about how fast he could run. One day, a tortoise asked him to race. The hare thought it was a joke. He agreed to the race. During the race, the hare ran very fast. He was winning. He thought he had time for a nap. He lay down and went to sleep. The tortoise passed the hare and won the race.

1 Who made the pictures?

① author

② illustrator

③ reader

2 What does the word *speedy* tell?

① where the hare is

② what the hare looks like

③ how the hare moves

3 How does the tortoise feel at the end?

① happy

② mad

③ sad

4 Why does the tortoise win?

① The hare naps.

② The hare gets lost.

③ The hare falls over.

5 What does the hare think the race will be like?

① easy

② hard

③ long

The Castle
by Tori North

Andrew loved to play with his blocks. He would build things with them every day.

One Sunday, he built a huge castle. It was very tall. It had a big tower. It took him a long time to build. Andrew was proud of his castle.

Photo by Jessica Lee

1. Who is the author?

　① Andrew

　② Tori North

　③ Jessica Lee

2. Which word tells how the castle looks?

　① play

　② built

　③ huge

3 What does Andrew make the castle from?

① blocks

② bricks

③ sand

4 When does Andrew make the castle?

① Friday

② Saturday

③ Sunday

5 Which word tells that Andrew thinks he did a good job?

① long

② proud

③ tall

Raindrops

Raindrops fall from the sky,
With a pitter-patter sound.
They make splashes when they fall,
On the ground, on the ground.

The flowers drink them up,
And grow tall and strong.
And when the rain stops, we look up,
And see a rainbow long.

1 Which two words rhyme?

① sky and fall

② sound and ground

③ flowers and drink

2 Which word rhymes with *strong*?

① long

② stops

③ tall

3   Which line tells what you hear?

   ①   With a pitter-patter sound.

   ②   They make splashes when they fall,

   ③   On the ground, on the ground.

4   What drinks up the water?

   ①   cats

   ②   flowers

   ③   kids

5   What is the poem about?

   ①   how plants grow

   ②   a rainy day

   ③   what rainbows are

Bonus Vocabulary Practice

Write a sentence using each word listed below.

1. book

_____

2. name

_____

3. bus

_____

4. sing

_____

Star Practice Exercises

Set 9

Reading Informational Texts

Instructions

Read each question carefully.

Each question has three answer choices.

Fill in the circle for the correct answer.

Bees

A bee is an insect. Bees have two wings and six legs. Bees are important. They help plants grow by pollinating them. They also make honey. Honey is so yummy!

Bees make sweet honey for us to eat! Yum!

1   What does the photo show?

   ①   where bees live

   ②   what bees make

   ③   how bees look

2   How many legs does a bee have?

   ①   2

   ②   6

   ③   8

3 Which detail is NOT a fact?

① Bees are insects.

② Bees make honey.

③ Honey is yummy.

4 What does the word *sweet* tell about honey?

① how it feels

② how it looks

③ how it tastes

5 Why are bees important?

① They feed animals.

② They fly around.

③ They help plants grow.

How to Make a Grilled Cheese Sandwich

1. Get two slices of bread and a slice of cheese.

2. Put the cheese between the two slices of bread.

3. Heat a frying pan on the stove.

4. Put the sandwich in the frying pan. Cook until the cheese is melted. The bread will be golden brown.

This looks so tasty!

1   What does the text teach people to do?

     ①   build something

     ②   cook something

     ③   fix something

2   What is the sandwich cooked in?

     ①   oven

     ②   frying pan

     ③   toaster

3   The caption says that the sandwich is tasty. What is this?

   ①   a fact

   ②   an opinion

   ③   a question

4   What do the words "golden brown" tell about the sandwich?

   ①   how it looks

   ②   how it smells

   ③   how it tastes

5   Which item is NOT needed?

   ①   bread

   ②   cheese

   ③   tomato

Keep the Park Clean!

We should put our trash in a trash can. We should never leave it on the ground. The trash will make the park look dirty. It can also harm animals. So, let's keep our park clean. Let's all pick up our trash.

1 What does the art show?

① why trash looks bad

② where to put trash

③ how much trash there is

2 What can the trash harm?

① animals

② kids

③ water

3 What is the text doing?

① giving facts

② asking people to do something

③ telling a story

4 Which word tells how the park could look?

① ground

② dirty

③ harm

5 What does the author want people to do?

① make less trash

② pick up trash they see

③ put trash in a trash can

Being a Farmer

I am a farmer. I grow lots of crops. I also take care of animals. I have cows and chickens. I sell the crops I grow. I also sell the milk and the eggs. Being a farmer is hard work. But it is also a great way to live.

1. How does the farmer look in the photo?

    ① happy

    ② mad

    ③ tired

2. Which food is NOT one the farmer sells?

    ① eggs

    ② honey

    ③ milk

3 Which sentence is a fact?

① I sell the crops I grow.

② Being a farmer is hard work.

③ But it is also a great way to live.

4 What do the words "lots of" tell about the crops?

① where they are

② how many there are

③ what color they are

5 What animals does the farmer have?

① cows and chickens

② pigs and ducks

③ sheep and goats

Bonus Vocabulary Practice

Write a sentence using each word listed below.

1. farm

_____

2. door

_____

3. yellow

_____

4. soon

_____

Star Practice Exercises

Set 10

Vocabulary

Instructions

Read each question carefully.

Each question has three answer choices.

Fill in the circle for the correct answer.

Vocabulary Quiz 1

1   I slid _____ the slide.

Which word goes on the line?

①   down

②   park

③   fast

2   The band was too _____.

Which word goes on the line?

①   playing

②   loud

③   song

3   The dog catches the stick.

What is the base word of catches?

① cat

② coat

③ catch

4   The cave was dim.

Which word means the same as dim?

① cold

② dark

③ scary

5   I watched a <u>film</u> on the TV.

What does *film* mean?

① friend

② movie

③ song

6   Read the words below.

circle
flower
square
triangle

Which word is not like the others?

① flower

② square

③ triangle

Vocabulary Quiz 2

1 I put a hat on my _____.

Which word goes on the line?

① head

② hot

③ sunny

2 We saw a _____ red beetle.

Which word goes on the line?

① crawl

② little

③ outside

3 We closed the front door.

Which word has the same base word as *closed*?

① calling

② closing

③ crying

4 We were late. We had to hurry.

Which word means the same as *hurry*?

① cry

② rush

③ yell

5   The old road was bumpy.

What does *bumpy* mean?

① long

② scary

③ rough

6   Read the words below.

chair
desk
table

Which word could be added to the list?

① bed

② brown

③ bus

Vocabulary Quiz 3

1 I like to play with _____ dog.

Which word goes on the line?

① catch

② my

③ all

2 The cheetah is the _____ animal.

Which word goes on the line?

① fastest

② run

③ cats

3 I enjoy riding my bike.

What is the base word of *riding*?

①   ride

②   read

③   run

4 The baby started to sob.

Which word means the same as *sob*?

①   crawl

②   cry

③   smile

5   I turned on the lamp. It started to glow.

What does *glow* mean?

① burn

② shake

③ shine

6   Read the words below.

hard
rough
soft
train

Which word is not like the others?

① rough

② soft

③ train

Vocabulary Quiz 4

1   I shooed the flies _____.

Which word goes on the line?

① away

② buzz

③ food

2   The car stopped at the _____ light.

Which word goes on the line?

① drive

② red

③ bus

3   The rain is <u>falling</u>.

Which word has the same base word as *falling*?

① falls

② fills

③ finds

4   The lion growled. It was <u>cranky</u>.

Which word means the same as *cranky*?

① mad

② noisy

③ silly

5   Jack got a pair of kittens.

How many kittens did Jack get?

① one

② two

③ ten

6   Read the words below.

fall
summer
winter

Which word could be added to the list?

① window

② puppy

③ spring

Bonus Vocabulary Practice

Write a sentence using each word listed below.

1. year

_____

2. room

_____

3. big

_____

4. shoe

_____

Star Practice Exercises

Set 11

Reading Prose and Poetry

Instructions
Read each question carefully.
Each question has three answer choices.
Fill in the circle for the correct answer.

Benny the Bear

A bear named Benny loved to eat sweet honey. He looked for beehives every day. He would climb up the trees. Then he would take a lick from the beehive. The bees didn't like this. They chased him away. Benny had to find a new food. He tried berries, fish, and nuts. He found out that he liked berries the best.

1 What did the illustrator do?

① draw the picture

② choose the title

③ write the words

2 What does the word *sweet* tell?

① how honey feels

② how honey looks

③ how honey tastes

3   What do the bees do?

   ①   chase Benny

   ②   laugh at Benny

   ③   sting Benny

4   What is the story about?

   ①   a bear making friends

   ②   a bear finding food

   ③   a bear being silly

5   What does Benny like most?

   ①   berries

   ②   fish

   ③   nuts

The Three Little Pigs

Three little pigs needed to build their own homes. The first pig built his house out of straw. The second pig built his house out of sticks. The third pig built his house out of bricks. A wolf came by. He blew down the house of straw. He blew down the house of sticks. But he could not blow down the house of bricks. The three pigs were safe in the house made of bricks.

1. Who would draw the picture?

    ① author

    ② illustrator

    ③ publisher

2. Which word tells how the pigs feel at the end?

    ① safe

    ② house

    ③ bricks

3 What does the first pig make his house from?

① sticks

② stones

③ straw

4 What is the brick house like?

① pretty

② small

③ strong

5 How do the pigs feel about the wolf?

① calm

② excited

③ scared

Bossy Boots
by Abby Carter

Mia was always telling people what to do. She was bossy. She had a loud voice. She told her sisters what to do. She told her friends what to do.

One day, a new girl told Mia what to do. Mia didn't like how it felt. She decided to stop being bossy. She learned to be a better friend.

Photo by Jo Evans

1. Who wrote the words?

    ① Mia

    ② Abby Carter

    ③ Jo Evans

2. What does the word *loud* tell about Mia?

    ① how she feels

    ② how she looks

    ③ how she sounds

3   Why does Mia change?

    ①   She is told what to do.

    ②   She has a fight.

    ③   She makes someone cry.

4   What is Mia's problem?

    ①   She is bossy.

    ②   She is lazy.

    ③   She is shy.

5   What is Mia like at the end?

    ①   a better friend

    ②   a smarter student

    ③   a meaner sister

The Moon

The moon is up so high,
In the night sky up above.
It shines so bright and silvery,
With a light that's full of love.

Sometimes round and sometimes thin,
But always beautiful to see.
We look up at the moon with a grin,
And make a wish for you and me.

1 Which words rhyme?

① thin and grin

② beautiful and see

③ you and me

2 What does the word *silvery* tell about the moon?

① its color

② its shape

③ its size

3   Which line tells where the moon is?

   ① In the night sky up above.
   ② It shines so bright and silvery,
   ③ With a light that's full of love.

4   What do the people do when they look at the moon?

   ① tell a story
   ② sing a song
   ③ make a wish

5   What does the poem say the moon always is?

   ① beautiful
   ② thin
   ③ round

Bonus Vocabulary Practice

Write a sentence using each word listed below.

1. tall

   _____

2. socks

   _____

3. five

   _____

4. nice

   _____

Star Practice Exercises

Set 12

Reading Informational Texts

Instructions

Read each question carefully.

Each question has three answer choices.

Fill in the circle for the correct answer.

Flowers

Flowers are parts of plants. They have petals. They come in different colors and shapes. Flowers can be grown in gardens. They also grow in the wild. Flowers make us happy when we see them. They smell so nice! They make a great gift.

Flowers have so many different shapes!

1. What does the art show?

    ① how flowers grow

    ② how flowers look

    ③ how flowers make people feel

2. What details does the text give?

    ① where flowers grow

    ② how to grow flowers

    ③ what flowers need to grow

3 Which detail is a fact?

① Flowers have petals.

② Flowers smell nice.

③ Flowers are great gifts.

4 Which word could describe what a flower looks like?

① red

② soft

③ sweet

5 How do flowers make people feel?

① happy

② sad

③ worried

Bubble Time!

1. Get some bubble solution and a wand.

2. Dip the wand in the bubble solution.

3. Hold the wand and blow gently.

4. Watch the bubble grow and float away.

1   Which step does the picture show?

    ①   Step 1

    ②   Step 2

    ③   Step 3

2   What do you do first?

    ①   shake the wand

    ②   dip the wand

    ③   blow on the wand

3   Which detail that could be added is a fact?

   ①   Bubbles are fun.

   ②   Bubbles are round.

   ③   Bubbles are pretty.

4   Which word tells how the bubbles move?

   ①   dip

   ②   float

   ③   gently

5   What is the text about?

   ①   how to blow bubbles

   ②   what bubbles look like

   ③   why people like bubbles

Brushing Your Teeth

We should always brush our teeth before bed. It helps keep our teeth and gums clean. Then you will have shiny white teeth. If we don't brush, our teeth might start to hurt. Plus, it's good to have a clean mouth before going to sleep. You should try to brush for 2 minutes.

1. When does the text say you should brush your teeth?

    ① at night

    ② after lunch

    ③ in the morning

2. How long should you brush for?

    ① 2 minutes

    ② 5 minutes

    ③ 10 minutes

3 What is the text mainly doing?

① giving facts

② telling opinions

③ asking questions

4 What does the word *shiny* tell about teeth?

① how they look

② how they feel

③ how they taste

5 What does the passage mainly tell?

① how to brush

② what to use to brush

③ why people should brush

Turtles

A turtle is a four-legged animal. Turtles have a hard shell. They move slowly. This is because their shells are heavy. They can live on land and in water. They are good swimmers. They hide inside their shells when they are scared.

1. What does the picture show a turtle doing?

    ① eating

    ② swimming

    ③ walking

2. When do turtles hide in their shells?

    ① when they are tired

    ② when they are scared

    ③ when they are bored

3   What does the passage mainly give?

   ①   facts

   ②   opinions

   ③   rules

4   What does the word *hard* tell about the shell?

   ①   how it feels

   ②   how it looks

   ③   how it sounds

5   Where can turtles live?

   ①   only on land

   ②   only in water

   ③   on land or in water

Bonus Vocabulary Practice

Write a sentence using each word listed below.

1. lion

_____

2. zoo

_____

3. park

_____

4. snow

_____

ANSWER KEY

About Florida's New English Language Arts Standards

Student learning and assessment in Florida is based on the skills listed in the new Benchmarks for Excellent Student Thinking, or B.E.S.T. The reading standards are divided into three areas: Reading Prose and Poetry, Reading Informational Text, and Reading Across Genres. The Star Reading tests also cover the skills in the Vocabulary section of the standards. The answer key that follows includes the skill assessed by each question.

Set 1 – Vocabulary

Vocabulary Quiz 1

Question	Answer	Skill
1	1	ELA.K.V.1.1: Use grade-level academic vocabulary appropriately in speaking and writing.
2	3	ELA.K.V.1.1: Use grade-level academic vocabulary appropriately in speaking and writing.
3	2	ELA.K.V.1.2: Ask and answer questions about unfamiliar words in grade-level content.
4	1	ELA.K.V.1.2: Ask and answer questions about unfamiliar words in grade-level content.
5	2	ELA.K.V.1.2: Ask and answer questions about unfamiliar words in grade-level content.
6	2	ELA.K.V.1.3: Identify and sort common words into basic categories, relating vocab to background knowledge.

Vocabulary Quiz 2

Question	Answer	Skill
1	1	ELA.K.V.1.1: Use grade-level academic vocabulary appropriately in speaking and writing.
2	2	ELA.K.V.1.1: Use grade-level academic vocabulary appropriately in speaking and writing.
3	2	ELA.K.V.1.2: Ask and answer questions about unfamiliar words in grade-level content.
4	1	ELA.K.V.1.2: Ask and answer questions about unfamiliar words in grade-level content.
5	2	ELA.K.V.1.2: Ask and answer questions about unfamiliar words in grade-level content.
6	3	ELA.K.V.1.3: Identify and sort common words into basic categories, relating vocab to background knowledge.

Vocabulary Quiz 3

Question	Answer	Skill
1	3	ELA.K.V.1.1: Use grade-level academic vocabulary appropriately in speaking and writing.
2	1	ELA.K.V.1.1: Use grade-level academic vocabulary appropriately in speaking and writing.
3	2	ELA.K.V.1.2: Ask and answer questions about unfamiliar words in grade-level content.
4	1	ELA.K.V.1.2: Ask and answer questions about unfamiliar words in grade-level content.
5	1	ELA.K.V.1.2: Ask and answer questions about unfamiliar words in grade-level content.
6	1	ELA.K.V.1.3: Identify and sort common words into basic categories, relating vocab to background knowledge.

Vocabulary Quiz 4

Question	Answer	Skill
1	2	ELA.K.V.1.1: Use grade-level academic vocabulary appropriately in speaking and writing.
2	1	ELA.K.V.1.1: Use grade-level academic vocabulary appropriately in speaking and writing.
3	3	ELA.K.V.1.2: Ask and answer questions about unfamiliar words in grade-level content.
4	3	ELA.K.V.1.2: Ask and answer questions about unfamiliar words in grade-level content.
5	1	ELA.K.V.1.2: Ask and answer questions about unfamiliar words in grade-level content.
6	3	ELA.K.V.1.3: Identify and sort common words into basic categories, relating vocab to background knowledge.

Set 2 – Reading Prose and Poetry

The Hungry Bunny

Question	Answer	Skill
1	2	ELA.K.R.1.3: Explain the roles of author and illustrator of a story.
2	3	ELA.K.R.3.1: Identify and explain descriptive words in text(s).
3	2	ELA.K.R.1.1: Describe the main character(s), setting, and important events in a story.
4	2	ELA.K.R.3.2: Retell a text orally to enhance comprehension.
5	1	ELA.K.R.3.3: Compare and contrast characters' experiences in stories.

The Spider and the Caterpillar

Question	Answer	Skill
1	1	ELA.K.R.1.3: Explain the roles of author and illustrator of a story.
2	2	ELA.K.R.3.1: Identify and explain descriptive words in text(s).
3	2	ELA.K.R.1.1: Describe the main character(s), setting, and important events in a story.
4	1	ELA.K.R.1.1: Describe the main character(s), setting, and important events in a story.
5	1	ELA.K.R.3.3: Compare and contrast characters' experiences in stories.

Dancing Girl

Question	Answer	Skill
1	1	ELA.K.R.1.3: Explain the roles of author and illustrator of a story.
2	3	ELA.K.R.3.1: Identify and explain descriptive words in text(s).
3	1	ELA.K.R.1.1: Describe the main character(s), setting, and important events in a story.
4	2	ELA.K.R.3.2: Retell a text orally to enhance comprehension.
5	1	ELA.K.R.3.3: Compare and contrast characters' experiences in stories.

Flowers

Question	Answer	Skill
1	3	ELA.K.R.1.4: Identify rhyme in a poem.
2	2	ELA.K.R.3.1: Identify and explain descriptive words in text(s).
3	2	ELA.K.R.1.1: Describe the main character(s), setting, and important events in a story.
4	2	ELA.K.R.3.1: Identify and explain descriptive words in text(s).
5	2	ELA.K.R.3.3: Compare and contrast characters' experiences in stories.

FAST Reading Skills Workbook, Daily Star Practice, Kindergarten

Set 3 – Reading Informational Texts

The Moon

Question	Answer	Skill
1	2	ELA.K.R.2.1: Use titles, headings, and illustrations to predict and confirm the topic of texts.
2	2	ELA.K.R.2.2: Identify the topic of and multiple details in a text.
3	3	ELA.K.R.2.4: Explain the difference between opinions and facts about a topic.
4	3	ELA.K.R.3.1: Identify and explain descriptive words in text(s).
5	1	ELA.K.R.3.2: Retell a text orally to enhance comprehension.

How to Brush Your Teeth

Question	Answer	Skill
1	3	ELA.K.R.2.1: Use titles, headings, and illustrations to predict and confirm the topic of texts.
2	2	ELA.K.R.2.2: Identify the topic of and multiple details in a text.
3	2	ELA.K.R.2.4: Explain the difference between opinions and facts about a topic.
4	3	ELA.K.R.3.1: Identify and explain descriptive words in text(s).
5	2	ELA.K.R.3.2: Retell a text orally to enhance comprehension.

About My Job

Question	Answer	Skill
1	3	ELA.K.R.2.1: Use titles, headings, and illustrations to predict and confirm the topic of texts.
2	3	ELA.K.R.2.2: Identify the topic of and multiple details in a text.
3	3	ELA.K.R.2.4: Explain the difference between opinions and facts about a topic.
4	3	ELA.K.R.3.1: Identify and explain descriptive words in text(s).
5	1	ELA.K.R.3.2: Retell a text orally to enhance comprehension.

Let's Put on Sunscreen

Question	Answer	Skill
1	3	ELA.K.R.2.1: Use titles, headings, and illustrations to predict and confirm the topic of texts.
2	1	ELA.K.R.2.2: Identify the topic of and multiple details in a text.
3	2	ELA.K.R.2.4: Explain the difference between opinions and facts about a topic.
4	1	ELA.K.R.3.1: Identify and explain descriptive words in text(s).
5	3	ELA.K.R.3.2: Retell a text orally to enhance comprehension.

Set 4 – Vocabulary

Vocabulary Quiz 1

Question	Answer	Skill
1	3	ELA.K.V.1.1: Use grade-level academic vocabulary appropriately in speaking and writing.
2	2	ELA.K.V.1.1: Use grade-level academic vocabulary appropriately in speaking and writing.
3	2	ELA.K.V.1.2: Ask and answer questions about unfamiliar words in grade-level content.
4	3	ELA.K.V.1.2: Ask and answer questions about unfamiliar words in grade-level content.
5	3	ELA.K.V.1.2: Ask and answer questions about unfamiliar words in grade-level content.
6	1	ELA.K.V.1.3: Identify and sort common words into basic categories, relating vocab to background knowledge.

Vocabulary Quiz 2

Question	Answer	Skill
1	2	ELA.K.V.1.1: Use grade-level academic vocabulary appropriately in speaking and writing.
2	1	ELA.K.V.1.1: Use grade-level academic vocabulary appropriately in speaking and writing.
3	2	ELA.K.V.1.2: Ask and answer questions about unfamiliar words in grade-level content.
4	1	ELA.K.V.1.2: Ask and answer questions about unfamiliar words in grade-level content.
5	2	ELA.K.V.1.2: Ask and answer questions about unfamiliar words in grade-level content.
6	3	ELA.K.V.1.3: Identify and sort common words into basic categories, relating vocab to background knowledge.

Vocabulary Quiz 3

Question	Answer	Skill
1	1	ELA.K.V.1.1: Use grade-level academic vocabulary appropriately in speaking and writing.
2	1	ELA.K.V.1.1: Use grade-level academic vocabulary appropriately in speaking and writing.
3	2	ELA.K.V.1.2: Ask and answer questions about unfamiliar words in grade-level content.
4	3	ELA.K.V.1.2: Ask and answer questions about unfamiliar words in grade-level content.
5	3	ELA.K.V.1.2: Ask and answer questions about unfamiliar words in grade-level content.
6	3	ELA.K.V.1.3: Identify and sort common words into basic categories, relating vocab to background knowledge.

Vocabulary Quiz 4

Question	Answer	Skill
1	1	ELA.K.V.1.1: Use grade-level academic vocabulary appropriately in speaking and writing.
2	1	ELA.K.V.1.1: Use grade-level academic vocabulary appropriately in speaking and writing.
3	1	ELA.K.V.1.2: Ask and answer questions about unfamiliar words in grade-level content.
4	3	ELA.K.V.1.2: Ask and answer questions about unfamiliar words in grade-level content.
5	3	ELA.K.V.1.2: Ask and answer questions about unfamiliar words in grade-level content.
6	1	ELA.K.V.1.3: Identify and sort common words into basic categories, relating vocab to background knowledge.

Set 5 – Reading Prose and Poetry

The Rainbow

Question	Answer	Skill
1	1	ELA.K.R.1.3: Explain the roles of author and illustrator of a story.
2	3	ELA.K.R.3.1: Identify and explain descriptive words in text(s).
3	1	ELA.K.R.1.1: Describe the main character(s), setting, and important events in a story.
4	2	ELA.K.R.3.2: Retell a text orally to enhance comprehension.
5	3	ELA.K.R.3.3: Compare and contrast characters' experiences in stories.

The Farmer and the Bird

Question	Answer	Skill
1	2	ELA.K.R.1.3: Explain the roles of author and illustrator of a story.
2	1	ELA.K.R.3.1: Identify and explain descriptive words in text(s).
3	2	ELA.K.R.1.1: Describe the main character(s), setting, and important events in a story.
4	1	ELA.K.R.3.2: Retell a text orally to enhance comprehension.
5	1	ELA.K.R.3.3: Compare and contrast characters' experiences in stories.

The Flashlight

Question	Answer	Skill
1		ELA.K.R.1.3: Explain the roles of author and illustrator of a story.
2		ELA.K.R.3.1: Identify and explain descriptive words in text(s).
3		ELA.K.R.1.1: Describe the main character(s), setting, and important events in a story.
4		ELA.K.R.1.1: Describe the main character(s), setting, and important events in a story.
5		ELA.K.R.3.3: Compare and contrast characters' experiences in stories.

The Sun

Question	Answer	Skill
1	3	ELA.K.R.1.4: Identify rhyme in a poem.
2	1	ELA.K.R.3.1: Identify and explain descriptive words in text(s).
3	3	ELA.K.R.1.1: Describe the main character(s), setting, and important events in a story.
4	1	ELA.K.R.3.2: Retell a text orally to enhance comprehension.
5	1	ELA.K.R.3.3: Compare and contrast characters' experiences in stories.

Set 6 – Reading Informational Texts

Birds

Question	Answer	Skill
1	1	ELA.K.R.2.1: Use titles, headings, and illustrations to predict and confirm the topic of texts.
2	1	ELA.K.R.2.2: Identify the topic of and multiple details in a text.
3	3	ELA.K.R.2.4: Explain the difference between opinions and facts about a topic.
4	2	ELA.K.R.3.1: Identify and explain descriptive words in text(s).
5	1	ELA.K.R.3.2: Retell a text orally to enhance comprehension.

How to Plant a Flower

Question	Answer	Skill
1	3	ELA.K.R.2.1: Use titles, headings, and illustrations to predict and confirm the topic of texts.
2	2	ELA.K.R.2.2: Identify the topic of and multiple details in a text.
3	2	ELA.K.R.2.4: Explain the difference between opinions and facts about a topic.
4	1	ELA.K.R.3.1: Identify and explain descriptive words in text(s).
5	1	ELA.K.R.3.2: Retell a text orally to enhance comprehension.

Henry Ford

Question	Answer	Skill
1	3	ELA.K.R.2.1: Use titles, headings, and illustrations to predict and confirm the topic of texts.
2	3	ELA.K.R.2.2: Identify the topic of and multiple details in a text.
3	3	ELA.K.R.2.4: Explain the difference between opinions and facts about a topic.
4	2	ELA.K.R.3.1: Identify and explain descriptive words in text(s).
5	1	ELA.K.R.3.2: Retell a text orally to enhance comprehension.

Playing the Piano

Question	Answer	Skill
1	1	ELA.K.R.2.1: Use titles, headings, and illustrations to predict and confirm the topic of texts.
2	2	ELA.K.R.2.2: Identify the topic of and multiple details in a text.
3	1	ELA.K.R.2.4: Explain the difference between opinions and facts about a topic.
4	1	ELA.K.R.3.1: Identify and explain descriptive words in text(s).
5	2	ELA.K.R.3.2: Retell a text orally to enhance comprehension.

Set 7 – Vocabulary

Vocabulary Quiz 1

Question	Answer	Skill
1	2	ELA.K.V.1.1: Use grade-level academic vocabulary appropriately in speaking and writing.
2	1	ELA.K.V.1.1: Use grade-level academic vocabulary appropriately in speaking and writing.
3	2	ELA.K.V.1.2: Ask and answer questions about unfamiliar words in grade-level content.
4	2	ELA.K.V.1.2: Ask and answer questions about unfamiliar words in grade-level content.
5	2	ELA.K.V.1.2: Ask and answer questions about unfamiliar words in grade-level content.
6	1	ELA.K.V.1.3: Identify and sort common words into basic categories, relating vocab to background knowledge.

Vocabulary Quiz 2

Question	Answer	Skill
1	3	ELA.K.V.1.1: Use grade-level academic vocabulary appropriately in speaking and writing.
2	1	ELA.K.V.1.1: Use grade-level academic vocabulary appropriately in speaking and writing.
3	2	ELA.K.V.1.2: Ask and answer questions about unfamiliar words in grade-level content.
4	2	ELA.K.V.1.2: Ask and answer questions about unfamiliar words in grade-level content.
5	1	ELA.K.V.1.2: Ask and answer questions about unfamiliar words in grade-level content.
6	1	ELA.K.V.1.3: Identify and sort common words into basic categories, relating vocab to background knowledge.

Vocabulary Quiz 3

Question	Answer	Skill
1	3	ELA.K.V.1.1: Use grade-level academic vocabulary appropriately in speaking and writing.
2	3	ELA.K.V.1.1: Use grade-level academic vocabulary appropriately in speaking and writing.
3	3	ELA.K.V.1.2: Ask and answer questions about unfamiliar words in grade-level content.
4	3	ELA.K.V.1.2: Ask and answer questions about unfamiliar words in grade-level content.
5	2	ELA.K.V.1.2: Ask and answer questions about unfamiliar words in grade-level content.
6	3	ELA.K.V.1.3: Identify and sort common words into basic categories, relating vocab to background knowledge.

Vocabulary Quiz 4

Question	Answer	Skill
1	1	ELA.K.V.1.1: Use grade-level academic vocabulary appropriately in speaking and writing.
2	3	ELA.K.V.1.1: Use grade-level academic vocabulary appropriately in speaking and writing.
3	2	ELA.K.V.1.2: Ask and answer questions about unfamiliar words in grade-level content.
4	2	ELA.K.V.1.2: Ask and answer questions about unfamiliar words in grade-level content.
5	2	ELA.K.V.1.2: Ask and answer questions about unfamiliar words in grade-level content.
6	1	ELA.K.V.1.3: Identify and sort common words into basic categories, relating vocab to background knowledge.

Set 8 – Reading Prose and Poetry

Friends

Question	Answer	Skill
1	3	ELA.K.R.1.3: Explain the roles of author and illustrator of a story.
2	1	ELA.K.R.3.1: Identify and explain descriptive words in text(s).
3	3	ELA.K.R.1.1: Describe the main character(s), setting, and important events in a story.
4	3	ELA.K.R.3.2: Retell a text orally to enhance comprehension.
5	1	ELA.K.R.3.3: Compare and contrast characters' experiences in stories.

The Tortoise and the Hare

Question	Answer	Skill
1	2	ELA.K.R.1.3: Explain the roles of author and illustrator of a story.
2	3	ELA.K.R.3.1: Identify and explain descriptive words in text(s).
3	1	ELA.K.R.1.1: Describe the main character(s), setting, and important events in a story.
4	1	ELA.K.R.3.2: Retell a text orally to enhance comprehension.
5	1	ELA.K.R.3.3: Compare and contrast characters' experiences in stories.

The Castle

Question	Answer	Skill
1	2	ELA.K.R.1.3: Explain the roles of author and illustrator of a story.
2	3	ELA.K.R.3.1: Identify and explain descriptive words in text(s).
3	1	ELA.K.R.1.1: Describe the main character(s), setting, and important events in a story.
4	3	ELA.K.R.1.1: Describe the main character(s), setting, and important events in a story.
5	2	ELA.K.R.3.3: Compare and contrast characters' experiences in stories.

Raindrops

Question	Answer	Skill
1	2	ELA.K.R.1.4: Identify rhyme in a poem.
2	1	ELA.K.R.1.4: Identify rhyme in a poem.
3	1	ELA.K.R.3.1: Identify and explain descriptive words in text(s).
4	2	ELA.K.R.3.2: Retell a text orally to enhance comprehension.
5	2	ELA.K.R.3.2: Retell a text orally to enhance comprehension.

Set 9 – Reading Informational Texts

Bees

Question	Answer	Skill
1	2	ELA.K.R.2.1: Use titles, headings, and illustrations to predict and confirm the topic of texts.
2	2	ELA.K.R.2.2: Identify the topic of and multiple details in a text.
3	3	ELA.K.R.2.4: Explain the difference between opinions and facts about a topic.
4	3	ELA.K.R.3.1: Identify and explain descriptive words in text(s).
5	3	ELA.K.R.3.2: Retell a text orally to enhance comprehension.

How to Make a Grilled Cheese Sandwich

Question	Answer	Skill
1	2	ELA.K.R.2.1: Use titles, headings, and illustrations to predict and confirm the topic of texts.
2	2	ELA.K.R.2.2: Identify the topic of and multiple details in a text.
3	2	ELA.K.R.2.4: Explain the difference between opinions and facts about a topic.
4	1	ELA.K.R.3.1: Identify and explain descriptive words in text(s).
5	3	ELA.K.R.3.2: Retell a text orally to enhance comprehension.

Keep the Park Clean!

Question	Answer	Skill
1	2	ELA.K.R.2.1: Use titles, headings, and illustrations to predict and confirm the topic of texts.
2	1	ELA.K.R.2.2: Identify the topic of and multiple details in a text.
3	2	ELA.K.R.2.4: Explain the difference between opinions and facts about a topic.
4	2	ELA.K.R.3.1: Identify and explain descriptive words in text(s).
5	3	ELA.K.R.3.2: Retell a text orally to enhance comprehension.

Being a Farmer

Question	Answer	Skill
1	1	ELA.K.R.2.1: Use titles, headings, and illustrations to predict and confirm the topic of texts.
2	2	ELA.K.R.2.2: Identify the topic of and multiple details in a text.
3	1	ELA.K.R.2.4: Explain the difference between opinions and facts about a topic.
4	2	ELA.K.R.3.1: Identify and explain descriptive words in text(s).
5	1	ELA.K.R.3.2: Retell a text orally to enhance comprehension.

Set 10 – Vocabulary

Vocabulary Quiz 1

Question	Answer	Skill
1	1	ELA.K.V.1.1: Use grade-level academic vocabulary appropriately in speaking and writing.
2	2	ELA.K.V.1.1: Use grade-level academic vocabulary appropriately in speaking and writing.
3	3	ELA.K.V.1.2: Ask and answer questions about unfamiliar words in grade-level content.
4	2	ELA.K.V.1.2: Ask and answer questions about unfamiliar words in grade-level content.
5	2	ELA.K.V.1.2: Ask and answer questions about unfamiliar words in grade-level content.
6	1	ELA.K.V.1.3: Identify and sort common words into basic categories, relating vocab to background knowledge.

Vocabulary Quiz 2

Question	Answer	Skill
1	1	ELA.K.V.1.1: Use grade-level academic vocabulary appropriately in speaking and writing.
2	2	ELA.K.V.1.1: Use grade-level academic vocabulary appropriately in speaking and writing.
3	2	ELA.K.V.1.2: Ask and answer questions about unfamiliar words in grade-level content.
4	2	ELA.K.V.1.2: Ask and answer questions about unfamiliar words in grade-level content.
5	3	ELA.K.V.1.2: Ask and answer questions about unfamiliar words in grade-level content.
6	1	ELA.K.V.1.3: Identify and sort common words into basic categories, relating vocab to background knowledge.

Vocabulary Quiz 3

Question	Answer	Skill
1	2	ELA.K.V.1.1: Use grade-level academic vocabulary appropriately in speaking and writing.
2	1	ELA.K.V.1.1: Use grade-level academic vocabulary appropriately in speaking and writing.
3	1	ELA.K.V.1.2: Ask and answer questions about unfamiliar words in grade-level content.
4	2	ELA.K.V.1.2: Ask and answer questions about unfamiliar words in grade-level content.
5	3	ELA.K.V.1.2: Ask and answer questions about unfamiliar words in grade-level content.
6	3	ELA.K.V.1.3: Identify and sort common words into basic categories, relating vocab to background knowledge.

Vocabulary Quiz 4

Question	Answer	Skill
1	1	ELA.K.V.1.1: Use grade-level academic vocabulary appropriately in speaking and writing.
2	2	ELA.K.V.1.1: Use grade-level academic vocabulary appropriately in speaking and writing.
3	1	ELA.K.V.1.2: Ask and answer questions about unfamiliar words in grade-level content.
4	1	ELA.K.V.1.2: Ask and answer questions about unfamiliar words in grade-level content.
5	2	ELA.K.V.1.2: Ask and answer questions about unfamiliar words in grade-level content.
6	3	ELA.K.V.1.3: Identify and sort common words into basic categories, relating vocab to background knowledge.

Set 11 – Reading Prose and Poetry

Benny the Bear

Question	Answer	Skill
1	1	ELA.K.R.1.3: Explain the roles of author and illustrator of a story.
2	3	ELA.K.R.3.1: Identify and explain descriptive words in text(s).
3	1	ELA.K.R.1.1: Describe the main character(s), setting, and important events in a story.
4	2	ELA.K.R.3.2: Retell a text orally to enhance comprehension.
5	1	ELA.K.R.3.3: Compare and contrast characters' experiences in stories.

The Three Little Pigs

Question	Answer	Skill
1	2	ELA.K.R.1.3: Explain the roles of author and illustrator of a story.
2	1	ELA.K.R.3.1: Identify and explain descriptive words in text(s).
3	3	ELA.K.R.1.1: Describe the main character(s), setting, and important events in a story.
4	3	ELA.K.R.3.2: Retell a text orally to enhance comprehension.
5	3	ELA.K.R.3.3: Compare and contrast characters' experiences in stories.

Bossy Boots

Question	Answer	Skill
1	2	ELA.K.R.1.3: Explain the roles of author and illustrator of a story.
2	3	ELA.K.R.3.1: Identify and explain descriptive words in text(s).
3	1	ELA.K.R.1.1: Describe the main character(s), setting, and important events in a story.
4	1	ELA.K.R.3.2: Retell a text orally to enhance comprehension.
5	1	ELA.K.R.3.3: Compare and contrast characters' experiences in stories.

The Moon

Question	Answer	Skill
1	1	ELA.K.R.1.4: Identify rhyme in a poem.
2	1	ELA.K.R.3.1: Identify and explain descriptive words in text(s).
3	1	ELA.K.R.1.1: Describe the main character(s), setting, and important events in a story.
4	3	ELA.K.R.3.2: Retell a text orally to enhance comprehension.
5	1	ELA.K.R.3.2: Retell a text orally to enhance comprehension.

Set 12 – Reading Informational Texts

Flowers

Question	Answer	Skill
1	2	ELA.K.R.2.1: Use titles, headings, and illustrations to predict and confirm the topic of texts.
2	1	ELA.K.R.2.2: Identify the topic of and multiple details in a text.
3	1	ELA.K.R.2.4: Explain the difference between opinions and facts about a topic.
4	1	ELA.K.R.3.1: Identify and explain descriptive words in text(s).
5	1	ELA.K.R.3.2: Retell a text orally to enhance comprehension.

Bubble Time!

Question	Answer	Skill
1	3	ELA.K.R.2.1: Use titles, headings, and illustrations to predict and confirm the topic of texts.
2	2	ELA.K.R.2.2: Identify the topic of and multiple details in a text.
3	2	ELA.K.R.2.4: Explain the difference between opinions and facts about a topic.
4	3	ELA.K.R.3.1: Identify and explain descriptive words in text(s).
5	1	ELA.K.R.3.2: Retell a text orally to enhance comprehension.

Brushing Your Teeth

Question	Answer	Skill
1	1	ELA.K.R.2.1: Use titles, headings, and illustrations to predict and confirm the topic of texts.
2	1	ELA.K.R.2.2: Identify the topic of and multiple details in a text.
3	2	ELA.K.R.2.4: Explain the difference between opinions and facts about a topic.
4	1	ELA.K.R.3.1: Identify and explain descriptive words in text(s).
5	3	ELA.K.R.3.2: Retell a text orally to enhance comprehension.

Turtles

Question	Answer	Skill
1	2	ELA.K.R.2.1: Use titles, headings, and illustrations to predict and confirm the topic of texts.
2	2	ELA.K.R.2.2: Identify the topic of and multiple details in a text.
3	1	ELA.K.R.2.4: Explain the difference between opinions and facts about a topic.
4	1	ELA.K.R.3.1: Identify and explain descriptive words in text(s).
5	3	ELA.K.R.3.2: Retell a text orally to enhance comprehension.

Made in United States
Orlando, FL
27 April 2023